GET REAL

Having a Ball

by PHiL Kettle

ILLustrated by MeLiSSa Webb

Get Real
Having a Ball

Written by Phil Kettle
Illustrations by Melissa Webb
Character design by David Dunstan

Published by
Macmillan Education Australia Pty Ltd
Level 1, 15–19 Claremont Street, South Yarra,
Victoria 3141
www.macmillan.com.au

Edited by Emma Short

Designed by Jenny Lindstedt,
Goanna Graphics (Vic) Pty Ltd

Printed in China
10 9 8 7 6 5 4 3 2 1

ISBN: (pack) 9781420291094

ISBN: 9781420290851

Contents

Introduction

Say hello to Harry Harvard and Jesse Harrison. The one on the left wearing a crash helmet, a chest protector, knee pads and elbow pads is Harry. The one on the right wearing a crash helmet, a chest protector, knee pads and elbow pads is Jesse.

And why are Harry and Jesse wearing crash helmets, chest protectors, knee pads and elbow pads? Because they're way back in prehistoric time, helping Rocky Rockman's Rock Village team win the annual rockball challenge match against Pebble Village, of course.

And if you didn't know that, you might want to read another book in this series, *Rockball*, before you start this one.

Get it? Got it? Good!

Chapter One

A Most Unusual Day

Harry and Jesse were *not* speeding through Average Park on their skateboards after school, or heading for their tree house as usual. They were *not* slowly making their way towards Average Primary School, ready for another day of playing pranks and tricks either. They were *not* laughing at their own jokes, and they were *not* writing lines or spending time in Principal Dorking's office.

Harry and Jesse had invited Mrs Payne and all the students in her Grade Six class to travel back in time. Their friend, the prehistoric caveman Rocky Rockman, needed more players for his rockball team. This would help his team (Rock Village) beat its arch rival (Pebble Town) in the annual rockball challenge.

Most of the Grade Six students had sat and listened in stunned silence. None of them had heard of rockball before... or Rock Village... or Pebble Town. And none of them had travelled back in time before either.

"Is there food involved?" Lenny 'the Stink' Edwards had asked.

"Yes," Jesse had replied.

So Lenny and the rest of the students had agreed to join in the fun. But it turned out that Principal Dorking and Samantha Smithers had been listening outside the door of Mrs Payne's Grade Six classroom. Jesse and Harry had activated the time machine and *everyone,* including Principal Dorking and Samantha Smithers, had been transported back to Rocky's cave in Rock Village.

ANOTHER NOTE FROM THE AUTHOR

So now you know what happened, even if you
didn't read that other book called **Rockball**.

Everyone, including Mrs Payne, Lenny `the Stink`
Edwards, Principal Dorking and Samantha
Smithers found themselves back in
prehistoric time with Harry, Jesse and
Rocky Rockman. Of course, this
could only be...

Chapter Two

A Bad Idea

Rocky Rockman and the rest of the rockball team were really excited to see Harry and Jesse and the rest of the Average citizens in the Rock Village team uniform. Harry and Jesse were really excited too. But the rest of the Average citizens were not so excited. Some looked terrified, some looked bored and some looked very angry indeed.

"I'm starting to think that this is a very bad idea," said Jesse.

"I think I agree," said Harry.

In a flash, Jesse had pulled out the remote control and programmed their destination ...

Location:
Mrs Payne's Grade Six classroom

Time:
About a zillion years from now, but five minutes before we left

"They'll never even know they were here..." Jesse said with a giggle. "One... *two*...THREE!"

And in another flash, the rest of the Average citizens were gone again.

"Hey," said Rocky Rockman. "What just happened to our team?" In that same flash, the big, rugged smile had disappeared from his big, rugged face.

"Don't worry, Rocky," said Jesse with a grin. "We don't need them. You've still got us!"

"I suppose so," said Rocky, starting to panic. "But I think we could have used the extra help."

"Don't worry, Rocky," laughed Harry. "Rock Village will win the annual rockball challenge, you'll see. "

"How can you be so sure?" asked Rocky.

"Because Jesse and I have plenty of sporting experience…" replied Harry, with a wink and a nod.

Author warning

The following chapter will be

very

long!

Chapter Three

Talking Tactics

Rocky Rockman was now feeling just a little less nervous than he was a few moments ago. "Maybe it's time to talk tactics," he said to the rest of the team.

"Great idea," said Jesse.

"Yes, tactics are very important," said Harry.

"But first can you remind us exactly how to play rockball again?" asked Jesse and Harry together.

Just in case you didn't have time
to read that other book I mentioned at the
start of this one, this is how you play rockball:

- Kick the rockball around a field and try
  to get goals.

- Try not to hurt your feet (because a
  rockball is just a big rock sewn inside
  a piece of dinosaur skin).

- The team that scores the most goals,
  and has the most players that are still
  standing at the end of the game, wins.

Cavemen train by banging their heads against
the walls of their caves. When their heads
stop hurting, they know they are
ready to play.

"That all sounds great," said Jesse, looking a little worried. "But I really think we need to change the way you train."

"And I really think that our list of safety equipment might help," finished Harry.

CRASH HELMETS

KNEE PADS

ELBOW PADS

CHEST PROTECTORS

SHIN GUARDS

STEEL-CAPPED SOCCER BOOTS

LARGE BOX OF BAND-AIDS

A REMINDER FROM THE AUTHOR

I know it might be hard to remember everything that happened in that other story, **Rockball**, so that's why I'm helping you along. And here's another bit I have to help you with.

You probably remember that Hugo and Howard are Jesse and Harry's alien friends from Planet Snoz. And if you don't remember this, you probably need to read another two books in this series, **Planet Snoz** and **Just Another Day**.

You might also remember that some time ago, Jesse and Harry had helped lead the Planet Snoz soccer team to a 400-nil victory over their arch rivals from Planet Dogsbreath. President Poobah of Planet Snoz was

SO
impressed,

he awarded Harry and Jesse

the electronic key card to Planet Snoz!

And you might also remember that Hugo and Howard had recently heard a rumour that their favourite Average earthlings were going back in time. Howard and Hugo had decided that they wanted to go too. So they had recently found themselves about a zillion years ago in prehistoric time, standing outside Rocky Rockman's cave with Harry, Jesse and Rocky.

"I think we should get out of the cold and into your cave," Hugo had said.

"Before our noses freeze and drop off," Howard had said.

"Come on everybody," Rocky had said. "Let's go inside."

So now Hugo and Howard were talking tactics with the rest of the Rock Village rockball team inside Rocky Rockman's cave.

"What we need…" said Howard.

"…is a really, *really*, REALLY good plan!" finished Hugo.

"It has to be so good that the Pebble Town players will crumble into gravel with no hope of winning!" said Harry.

"Yes," nodded Jesse. "That's exactly the kind of plan that we need."

About fifteen seconds later…

I think I've got it!

"But first," he continued, reaching for the remote control for the time machine, "Jesse and I need to take a little trip into the immediate future."

Harry programmed their destination into the time machine.

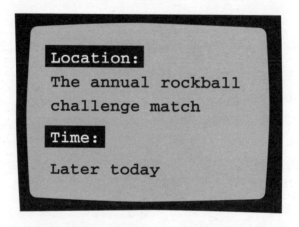

Location:
The annual rockball challenge match

Time:
Later today

"Don't worry, we'll be back very soon," he told the rest of the Rock Village rockball team.

"One…*two*…THREE!" Jesse shouted, and Harry pressed the red button.

Rocky

Howard

Hugo

33

Harry and Jesse found themselves standing on the field in the middle of the annual rockball challenge match.

"Wow, look at the crowd. They're going wild," said Harry, looking around.

"And look at that Pebble Town player running straight towards me!" said Jesse, jumping out of the way just in time.

"Phew," gasped Harry. "If he'd have hit you, you'd be flatter than Lenny 'the Stink' Edwards's cat after it was run over by a car and turned into a door mat!"

PEBBLE TOWN 6

ROCK VILLAGE 0

"Wow, look at the score," said Harry, pointing at the scoreboard. "Pebble Town has kicked six goals to zero and the match is almost over!"

The Pebble Town players looked fresh and full of energy. The Rock Village players were holding their sore feet and rubbing their sore heads. Some of them were lying on the ground.

"It's not looking good, Harry" said Jesse, shaking his head. "I don't know if Rock Village can win from here."

"You're right, Jesse," Harry replied. "But don't give up hope. Do you remember when we first found our time machine? We used it to travel to the future and watch the World Cup of Soccer *before* it actually happened."

"Of course I remember," said Jesse. "That was the most fun I've

 had!"

"And not only did we watch the match, we actually changed the result!" Harry finished.

Jesse's eyes lit up. "Hey Harry," he said slowly. "Now I think I'm really starting to get your plan..."

A REMINDER FROM THE AUTHOR

You may remember the very first time Harry and Jesse used their time machine. One minute they were in their tree house and the next minute they were in France, standing in the middle of Frog Park. And not only were they standing in the middle of Frog Park. They were also standing in the middle of the final of the World Cup of Soccer, between Australia and France.

The boys used the time machine to freeze time, sent the French team totally around the twist, and helped Australia to victory!

Just in case you didn't already notice, that was the

LONGEST

chapter ever. So don't blink, because I'm going to make the next few chapters

so short

that if you blink, you might miss them!

Chapter four

The Plan

Jesse and Harry knew what they had to do. Harry reached out his hand and pressed the purple button on the remote control for the time machine. Suddenly everything slowed down around them. It seemed as if the game had gone into slow motion, and after a few seconds it wound down to a complete halt. The players were spread across the field like statues.

First, Jesse and Harry re-arranged the Pebble Town team. Harry tied the two biggest players together by their beards. Then he put a big dinosaur bone just in front of another player's feet.

Meanwhile, Jesse pulled the goalkeeper's fur jumper over his head.

"This is the most fun I've  had since the last time I had the most fun I've  had," Harry laughed.

"I know what you mean," said Jesse. "This is the *new* most fun I've

had. In fact, I'm having a ball!"

Finally, the boys worked together to roll the remaining Pebble Town players into a pile in the middle of the field.

Next, Jesse and Harry re-arranged
the Rock Village team. They picked up
the sad and sorry players, including
themselves. Then they put them in a line
from one end of the field to the other.
They prodded and poked their faces until
they looked fierce and powerful. Then
they took the rock out of the rockball to
make it much softer and lighter. And
finally, they put the softer lighter rockball
just in front of Rocky Rockman's foot.

Chapter five

Huh?

A NOTE FROM THE AUTHOR

This chapter is really nothing but an important warning, because I promised to keep the next few chapters short. But be warned – this warning is actually quite long!

Author Warning

If, when you read
something that makes
you laugh, you laugh

so hard

that you

lose total control

of your body, then may
I suggest that you

don't read the next
two chapters in bed!

Chapter Six

Action!

Harry and Jesse stood back to admire their work. It was time to re-start time and watch how the last five minutes of the game unfolded. The boys looked at each other and put their hands on the green button of the remote control for the time machine. They both took a deep breath.

"One...*two*...THREE!"

ANOTHER NOTE FROM THE AUTHOR

Well, I told you there were going to be a few

short chapters after Chapter Three, didn't I?

And now you can see that I was right.

But just to be different, I'll make the next

chapter a bit longer!

Chapter Seven

Five Minutes to Go

Welcome back to the annual ROCKBALL
CHALLENGE MATCH between Rock Village and
Pebble Town. I'm your commentator, T-Rex. The
score is 6-0 to Pebble Town and there's just five
minutes to go!

Rocky Rockman of Rock Village is about to take a kick. WHOOSH! The ball is flying straight up in the air like a rocket! I've never seen anything like it. All of a sudden it doesn't look heavy at all!

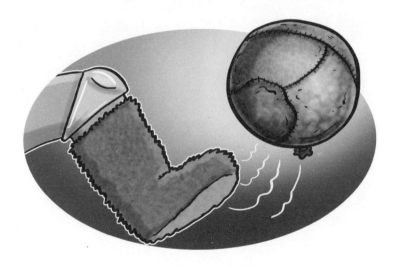

Oh my goodness, the ball is coming down now! Where will it land? Who will catch it? I can't believe what I'm seeing!

The Rock Village players can't believe what they're seeing either. At least I think they're Rock Village players... I've never seen cavemen like that before!

The ball is finally coming back down. Big Pebble and Large Pebble are both underneath it, waiting to take the catch. Big runs to the left, Large runs to the right – but wait! They've both fallen flat on their faces!

A few moments ago, the Rock Village team looked smashed. But suddenly they have a chance!

A Rock Village player has grabbed the ball and kicks it to another...

who passes it to another...

who kicks it to another...

who kicks it to another!

Now Rocky Rockman has the rockball. He tucks it under his arm and runs towards the goal. A Pebble Town player tries to stop him – but what's this? It looks like the Pebble Town player has tripped over a dinosaur bone. How did that get on the field?

Rocky Rockman keeps on running. He puts the ball on the ground, lines it up and drives it towards the goal.

The Pebble Town goalkeeper misses the ball! How did that happen? It must have been because he's pulled his jumper over his head!

Anyway, that's old news now. Rock Village has scored a goal and the crowd has really come to life!

Pebble Town is in **BIG** trouble. I think most of their players have given up. In fact, they seem to be tangled up in a pile in the middle of the field!

Rock Village can score - again and again and again and again and again and again!

And that's it, folks! The final siren has sounded.
Rock Village has won the annual rockball challenge!

Chapter eight

Let's Celebrate!

When Jesse and Harry had finished cheering, they grabbed the remote control for the time machine and returned to Rocky's cave.

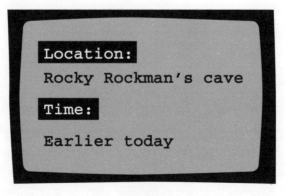

Location:
Rocky Rockman's cave
Time:
Earlier today

The rest of the team had lots of questions.

"How did it go?"

"Did the plan work?"

"Do we need to train harder?"

"Do we need any special skills?"

"Relax," said Harry, winking at Jesse. "There's no need to worry about a thing."

"I think this will be the best game of rockball that Rock Village ever plays," said Jesse, winking back at Harry.

"I hope so," said Rocky Rockman, looking *very* pleased. "And if you're right, let's take the trophy back to Average with us when we leave."

"Great idea," said Hugo and Howard. "And maybe you can bring it to Planet Snoz for a visit too!"

Prehistoric Daily News

ROCK VILLAGE STEALS VICTORY

By Scoop Stone

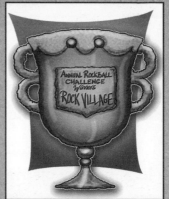

Cavemen arrived from all over the land today to watch the annual rockball challenge match between Rock Village and Pebble Town. When Pebble Town took a 6-0 lead, it looked like a landslide victory. But then the match took an incredible and unexplained turn. The Rock Village players were able to rock and roll their way back into the lead with seconds to go. They stole a famous victory.

Let's Write

Imagine if you were writing a story about Harry and Jesse, and their best prehistoric caveman friend, and they had just gone back to prehistoric time to play rockball. Would your story run smoothly? Would everything happen just as you thought it would when you made your story plan?

If you've already read the first series of *Get Real*, and I think you probably have, then you might remember that a writing adventure can be a lot like a real-life adventure. You might run into an obstacle that causes you to change direction in your story.

Use your imagination and pretend that you're on the Pebble Town rockball team playing against Harry, Jesse, Rocky Rockman and the rest of the Rock Village team. Pebble Town is ahead, 6-0, and it looks like a landslide victory is coming up. But then the match takes an incredible and unexplained turn...

Write about all the obstacles the Pebble Town team have to overcome. Can they do it, or will Rock Village be able to steal victory? It's not my story anymore – it's your story, so the result is up to you. And remember, obstacles and complications are just another part of the writing adventure. Good luck!

GO ROCKS!

PLAY WELL PEBBLES!

Jesse and Harry Present

About the Author

Jesse: Hey Phil, have you ever played football with something that wasn't a football?

Phil: Yes I have. Once I rolled up an old newspaper and tied it with a string. My friend and I kicked it around the garden.

Jesse: That sounds like a weird football to me.

Phil: It was. And when we got sick of kicking it, we unwrapped it again and read it.

Jesse: I bet I know what section of the newspaper you read first.

Phil: What section is that?

Jesse: The sports section, of course!

Phil: You're wrong there, Jesse.

Jesse: So what section did you read first?

Phil: The comics!

About the Illustrator

Harry: Hey Melissa, did you ever play football when you were young?

Melissa: Are you kidding? I'd be as good at football as I am at rockball!

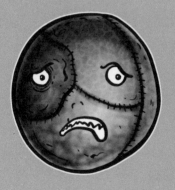

Word-up!

Blowie: a large and very noisy fly

Blowy: windy

The bee's knees: the best, the most perfect, the greatest ever

Elbow grease: hard work

A Laugh a Minute!

What did the ground say to the earthquake?
You crack me up!

What did the pencil sharpener say to the pencil?
Stop going in circles and get to the point!

How does a barber cut the moon's hair?
E-clipse it!

What happened when the wheel was invented?
It caused a revolution.

Why do kangaroo mums hate bad weather?
Because their joeys have to play inside.

Other Titles in the Series